BRITAIN IN OLD PHC

GREAT YARMOUTH REVISITED

MICHAEL TEUN

SUTTON PUBLISHING LIMITED

Sutton Publishing Limited
Phoenix Mill · Thrupp · Stroud
Gloucestershire · GL5 2BU

First published 1996

Cover photographs: front: Gorleston Carnival, 4 July 1923; back: Star Supply Stores, King Street. Page 1: King Street looking towards Market Place, *c.* 1903. Taken from the top of an electric tram.

British Library Cataloguing in Publication Data
A catalogue record for this book is available from the British Library.

ISBN 0-7509-1154-9

Typeset in 10/12 Perpetua.
Typesetting and origination by
Sutton Publishing Limited.
Printed in Great Britain by
Ebenezer Baylis, Worcester.

I dedicate this to you, Susanne

Friars Lane, *c.* 1969. Mr Carter's fried fish shop was a favourite with people in the Middlegate Street area. A request for 'two and one' in the 1930s would result in a large piece of fish and as big a pennyworth of chips as you would get for 50p today. By 1963 Mr Ellis had taken over the business. The Gedge family traded next door. Robert Gedge, a saddler, started in Friars Lane in the early 1890s, followed by Gregory Gedge by the early 1930s. Both of these buildings were demolished in the late 1960s to make way for the fire station, which has been standing on the site to this day.

CONTENTS

INTRODUCTION

To a large extent this second volume has materialized because of the encouragement and further information given to me by people who, once again, wish to be reminded of 'the good old days'. Through their generosity we can continue our journey back in time walking the streets so familiar to our fathers and forefathers. The present generation is growing up surrounded by modern flats and wide streets. There once stood rows so narrow that from their windows people from one side could almost shake hands with people on the other. Times have changed since the residents carried their Sunday joints to a bakery for roasting, the grand price of which was just 2d. The baker also offered dumplings ready for cooking – two dumplings for 1½d. Meanwhile in one street they had the choice of nearly twenty public houses from which could be fetched beer in jugs.

The passage of time has certainly erased everything that would remind us of the poverty, long working hours and unemployment in bygone days when life was so hard. The flats and maisonettes built on the old Middlegate are a far cry from the overcrowding, crude sanitation and lack of amenities suffered by the tenants of the houses before the Second World War. As many as 103 dwellings stood to the acre, served only by cold water standpipes, each shared by several households.

At this time the sign of the pawnbroker's shop was a familiar sight in any reasonable sized town. Memories are still fresh of people queuing to hock items of all descriptions: from bed linen to washing mangles. People too proud to enter a pawn shop even tipped a 'pledge runner' to take their possessions in for them. A tale is told of a local character who would frequent the pawnbrokers every Saturday lunchtime. He was a carpenter, and he pledged his tools for the weekend, but was always the first in the queue to redeem them early on the Monday morning. One of the last of such traders in Great Yarmouth was Bartram's jewellers and pawnbrokers of 132 King Street.

Today we have hot water systems and bathrooms. In days past when a wash was required, a kettle was boiled and refilled many times, or the copper was heated and emptied to fill the old tin bath. We can also compare our well-lit homes of today with the dark rooms of the old smaller row houses, the residents of which were compelled to use some form of artificial lighting from the time they arose until the time they retired in the evening.

How people made the best out of these living conditions and remained comparatively happy in their sphere of life is difficult to conceive, but they were, as many as the townsfolk I have talked to can confirm. These so-called slums were in fact their castles. However, scrupulously clean kitchens could not disguise the fact that many of the walls were being held together by wallpaper; that a big varnished post in one corner was holding up a wooden beam, thus preventing the ceiling from falling down; that the dark stain that threw up the gaudy colours of the wallpaper was indeed a damp patch. It is difficult to imagine how wives took such meticulous care over their homes, which were in fact crumbling to pieces and, in the late 1930s, were under the ban of demolition orders, but these little rooms held all of their dreams and secrets. The shiny brass ornaments on the mantelpiece were to them objects of beauty. The whole of family life revolved around these miserable surroundings.

It would be absolutely wrong to say that the entire row area consisted of slums. Many houses did indeed have to be demolished, but what caused annoyance was the wanton destruction of the whole area, ruining a scheme that had been so successful hundreds of years ago. A great part of the area had been scheduled for clearance prior to 1939, but the outbreak of hostilities put an end to any immediate hope of improvements. In April 1941, for example, Middlegate Street and the surrounding rows suffered severely in air-raids. In a few seconds, more houses were wrecked than scores of demolition experts could have destroyed in a matter of months. Further raids caused more destruction, and later in the war part of this area was used as a training area for house-to-house fighting. Thus by the end of the war, few of the buildings were considered to be worth preserving, resulting in the whole district – including and extending beyond the original clearance areas – becoming one of the several reconstruction sites in the town.

A book of this nature could never have been completed without the generous help of a large number of people, to whom I am extremely grateful. During the last year I have corresponded with Mr Clarke, who was born in 1932 in Middlegate Street, and who is now living in Colchester. His family occupied the living quarters of Miss Dyball's drapery shop (42a Middlegate Street). The bedrooms overlooked the street, but the entrance was found a short distance into Row 119. Opposite (11 Row 119) lived Robert Ebbage, who had a number of bicycles, which he hired out for a few pence a time. Mr Ebbage rode a three-wheeler bicycle with a large box on the front exactly like the old Walls ice-cream bikes. Whenever he rode past the end of the row he would honk his horn – one of the old types with a big rubber bulb. Sometimes he would honk it once, but mostly it was two or three times. When Mr Clarke asked his father why this was, he was told that it was Mr Ebbage's way of letting his wife know how many dumplings he wanted for dinner.

Next door in Middlegate Street lived Harry Davis, the barber. He had a parrot that had a very foul mouth. Unfortunately the local children used to torment it to make it lose its temper and swear at them. If Harry nipped into the pub for a 'quick one' and a customer showed up in his shop, the parrot would often say: 'He's in the pub.' When Harry arrived he would make some excuse for his absence, but the parrot would say: 'Liar liar, you've been to the pub.' Harry would then threaten to kill the bird, which would scream: 'Murder, murder.'

Frank Mansi's ice-cream shop (148 Middlegate Street) could be seen from the Clarkes' window. Frank would sit in his living-room in shirt sleeves and waistcoat, with his jacket and black Italian hat nearby. Whenever a customer entered the shop he would put on his jacket and hat before returning to the shop and scooping out some ice-cream, creating a fine cornet to order. He would then again take off his jacket and hat and resume his position in his armchair to await the next customer.

During the Second World War, whenever the air-raid sirens sounded the Clarke family would cross the road to the Druids Arms and stay in the pub cellar until the raid was over. The children were given chocolate wafer biscuits and sometimes lemonade. It was the landlord of the Druids Arms, Edgar Aldous, who discovered the body of the murdered Horace Butcher.

In 1934 a well-known marine store dealer, Mr Horace Butcher, aged 68, was found dead with his head terribly battered. He was in his sitting-room, on a sofa, at the rear of his business premises at 151 Middlegate Street. His shop was said to have been one of the oldest in the street, with old-fashioned small-paned windows on each side of the door; while inside, the floor was covered with a miscellaneous confusion of assorted bottles, bones, rags and metal.

Butcher lived alone in these premises, which were at the corner of Row 112, and the fact that he was not seen in the early hours of this particular Tuesday morning aroused no suspicion, as at times he was a late riser. However, when he had not been seen by twelve o'clock, Mr Edgar Aldous began to feel that all was not well and gained entry by forcing the shop door. He soon discovered that his fears were well founded. On entering the shop he saw the gas light half on in the sitting-room at the rear, and blood on the floor of the dividing passage. Just inside the door of the sitting-room he found Butcher lying on the couch, obviously dead. Around his head was wound a bloodstained towel, and drawn over him were a pair of trousers and a waistcoat. On the floor lay a bloodstained 7 lb iron weight with hair sticking to it. The weight had probably been taken from the shop where Butcher kept his scales for weighing out the metal, and old rags and bones.

Deductions point to the fact that the attacker was on the premises when Butcher arrived home after his evening stroll. Whether the intent was robbery, or whether someone had a grudge and lay in wait for him is a matter of conjecture. It was suggested that perhaps a seaman was responsible for the crime – but to this day the murder remains an unsolved mystery.

However, this level of crime was a rare occurrence. Most doors could be left unlocked, and indeed were, while cars, bicycles and other property could also be left safely unattended. People were prepared to help both themselves and their neighbours – there were few social services then.

When you are pushing your trolley along the supermarket aisles today, negotiating other burdened shoppers, just try to imagine how much weekly grocery buying has changed since a few decades ago. Reps from stores similar to the long-gone Bussey's in Gorleston High Street visited our home weekly for a modest order. If you went out to buy the weekend provisions, it was to the Maypole, Home and Colonial or Clowes' and Becket and Pitcher – black-and-white tiled premises with highly polished brass scale weights, where very little was prepacked. Staff were quite adept at patting butter, neatly wrapping tasty cheese in greaseproof paper and folding the top of blue sugar bags.

Names of old traders that evoke nostalgia and are to be found in this book include the following: Delf and Sons of Middlegate Street; Middleton's of Broad Row; Hill's Restaurant in King Street; Carr's and Bond's both of the Market Row; Pagano's of Blackfriars Road; Wilson's in Middlegate Street. From these shops, a few coins could buy so much. From Harry Davis's fishing tackle and hairdressing shop in Middlegate, a penny ball of string and a halfpenny fish hook, together with a few herring picked up off the fishwharf, could equip you to go fishing. If you were feeling hungry, there were many fish shops, including Carter's on Friars Lane. A penny's worth of chips was available from the market, tea was a penny a cup and cakes could also be purchased for a penny each. Indeed, a penny went a long, long way.

In this book I should like to invite you to join me in some of Great Yarmouth's ancient backstreets, where once again we will visit the old shops and pubs, then take a walk along the seafront, where the sun always seemed to shine.

SECTION ONE

STREETS

A group of real 'Yarmouth bloaters' standing outside the New Fountain public house, 127 Middlegate Street, late 1920s. They look happy in their familiar surroundings. Note the infant in arms, who is turning to look at the cheery couple who have swapped hats for a laugh.

The Tolhouse, Middlegate Street, *c.* 1880. Note the police sign on the front. While the new police station (below) was being built, the police force moved temporarily into the Tolhouse.

The police station, Middlegate Street, at the corner of Row 76. This station eventually proved to be cramped, ill-equipped and insanitary. Hot water had to be boiled in a copper downstairs and carried upstairs in buckets to fill a bath for the firemen when they returned from fires. The station was rebuilt in 1912 and is used today as council offices.

Middlegate Street. From left to right, just in view, Row 84 next to the Ship Tavern. The Ship, being one of the few old Middlegate Street buildings remaining today, was built as a private house by John Ireland, who was Mayor of Great Yarmouth in 1716. At 6 Middlegate Street, William Wigg sold fresh fish, with Joseph Niman, tailor, trading next door in the 1930s. Nos 8 and 9 follow on to the west end of Row 88.

Looking from Queen Street, 6 and 7 Middlegate Street. This photograph was taken after the Second World War and shows bomb damage. Note the early seventeenth-century gable end on no. 7.

View from South Quay on to the north end of Middlegate Street, 1950. The Ship public house, with the ambulance parked opposite near to the fire station, is to the left. The end of Row 88 is just left of the last shop, adjacent to the buildings that are in the process of being demolished. In the foreground is the old line of Row 92. The west side of the street has already been demolished.

The public library on the north side of Row 108, off Middlegate Street, early 1950s. Following damage in 1941, then again in 1942, the library was moved temporarily to 16/17 Hall Quay, which was formerly Clowes' grocery stores. It remained there until the new library was built on the original site, with the old entrance door opposite today's main entrance.

Middlegate Street, *c.* 1943. Henry Culley's grocer's shop (left) is at no. 28, next door to Mr Newton's draper's shop. Following on from Row 109, the shop to the far right was being run by Mrs Palmer in 1938. The sunlight in the foreground is shining down from Row 108, opposite.

Middlegate Street, in a view looking north, *c.* 1900. The chemist shop belonging to John Cutforth is seen on the left, with the dentist sign. The posters on the shop next door are the property of John High, billposter. The lady in black is passing the Friendly Societies Hall, whose sign is quite visible. This building later became the Salvation Army Hall. The next building, with the gable end to the road, is the Suffolk Tavern public house (see vol. 1, p. 92).

No. 161 Middlegate Street, 1945. Mr Eastoe moved to these premises temporarily after bomb damage to no. 172. John High's billposter can be seen to the right. Note also the posters on his shop. Bomb damage can be seen both to the Tolhouse and to the east end of Row 106.

Looking south from 67 Middlegate Street, *c.* 1943. Delf and Sons' wholesale grocer's shop is at no. 67. The west end of Row 135 is to the right. The gate was to cordon off part of Middlegate Street for training purposes during the Second World War.

Nos 40/41 Middlegate Street. This fine building stood on the north-west corner of Row 119. Built in 1534, it is depicted on Corbridge's Picture Map of Yarmouth dating from 1724, just after the front was bricked up in 1719. In 1938 Thomas Parke traded as an outfitter from these premises.

The police and fire station, Middlegate Street, *c.* 1912. In December 1911 the town council gave the go-ahead for the erection of a new police and fire station. Photographed here with the builders, the new construction looks almost completed.

Ewles Fish Shop, 73 Middlegate Street, *c.* 1920. These were the days when pink shrimps could be bought for 1*d* a pint.

Nos 117/118 Middlegate Street, *c.* 1944. Dennis Delf's grocer's shop is looking very sorry for itself. While it is undoubtedly the case that most of this area had to be redeveloped, the failure to preserve even one portion of a few rows must rank as the worst of this town's acts of post-war vandalism. Note the east end of Row 138 to the right.

No. 160 Middlegate Street, *c.* 1920. Known as Wilson's, these premises stood on the corner of Row 108. It was the last of the old Middlegate shops, the trading tastes of which were so numerous and varied that you could be supplied with anything from a grand piano to a tin tack and not be robbed. This shop survives today as a small café.

No. 130 Middlegate Street, *c.* 1925. Lark's hatter and outfitter. It was usual for these shops to be open from six in the morning to ten at night.

Howard Street South, *c.* 1960. To the left following on from the 'no waiting' sign is Mr Evans's electrical shop. Opposite is a well-known public house, The Blue House, which was purchased by Brett's in 1971. Note the brewery in the background and the postman with his basket on wheels.

Howard Street South, looking south, *c.* 1960. Hunt's soft drinks manufacturers is to the left. A pram can just be seen in Kelf's window on the right. Next is the shell-fish shop, which was owned by Mr Edwards, with the signs above. The east side was demolished in the late 1960s to make way for Palmer's car park.

A congested Howard Street South, late 1960s. The large building, which at this time was owned by Hunt's, was formerly the Black Swan public house. In 1868 the Hunt family moved from Norwich and took over the factory of Samuel Ives, which had been producing mineral water at 8 Howard Street South since the 1840s. For many years the firm produced its ginger beer in the traditional stone bottles. The business expanded with the further purchase of property on the east side of Howard Street South. The Corn Hall opposite was also purchased for the confectionery side of the business. The Howard Street factory closed in 1968 and the buildings were soon after demolished.

No. 13 Howard Street South, 1930s. The shop of Harry Bradbury was situated between Row 56 and Row 58.

No. 19 Howard Street South, *c.* 1920. Spanton's fish shop. Mrs Spanton is to the right. Note the sign advertising bloaters.

Nos 31/32 Howard Street South, 1910. Row 80 is to the far left, adjoining what was for many years a printer's shop – in the 1920s Blake's and in the 1930s Rippon's. The private house to the right survived until the late 1950s, then gave way to yet another car park.

Howard Street South, looking north towards the junction of Regent Street, *c.* 1923. Row 74 is plainly visible with the barrow at the end of Row 73. Row 74 was demolished to build the present-day arcade.

Howard Street South, in a view looking south. Kelf's, to the right, adjoins Edwards's shell-fish shop. The open space, with gates pushed open, is next door to the Corn Hall. The arch seen over the doorway of this building has somehow found its way to the present-day library, where it lies on the ground on its back, looking most undignified and out of place.

A street party in George Street in the 1930s, possibly to celebrate the coronation of George VI (see vol. 1, p. 52).

King Street, looking towards the Market Place, 1941. By Easter week 1941 the town was well used to the sounds of falling bombs. However, just after midnight on the night of 7/8 April the town underwent a heavy attack that lasted four nights. Jarrold's, shown with the upper storeys damaged, is to the left. Next door is the east end of Row 63, with Kerridge's, completely destroyed, on the right side. Palmer's men's shop at 41/42 Market Place, which escaped serious damage, is to the far right.

The corner of Fullers Hill and George Street, 1962. The north gable of this building fell and blocked Fullers Hill. These premises were demolished soon after.

King Street, looking south from the Market Place, before 1860. On the east side the sign 'Simpson' can be seen. In 1860 Messrs Biddlecombe and Boning purchased the drapers business of Mr Simpson. This was the birth of the later large department store. The corner building at 43 Market Place was the residence of Charles Dashwood, a surgeon. Next door, with blind extended, is another draper's shop, owned by William Livingston. Note the crossing where ladies could cross the road without dirtying their long dresses. The sign of a third draper in this area, Parson's, can just be seen to the right.

Nos 39/40 King Street, *c.* 1924. These are the showrooms of the Great Yarmouth Gas Company. A datestone from 1912 can be seen on the building, which, sadly, today is empty, its fate unknown. The large gas lamps outside the shop are clearly visible, and the filled-in holes from these can still be seen today. Row 114 is to the left of the showrooms.

The interior of the gas company showrooms. Note the gas cookers and the sign giving directions around the shop. To the right is a chair that was placed for customers' comfort and convenience, a usual practice in stores years ago.

No. 168 King Street. John Harbord, confectioner, in his shop doorway, *c.* 1875. Row 80 is to the left. By 1905 the business was in the hands of a Mr Hill.

No. 168 King Street, Hill's Restaurant, 1923. This was said to have been one of the finest restaurants in the Eastern Counties. Unfortunately the business was bombed out in the air-raid of April 1941. It did continue for a time, nearer the Market Place, above Burton's the tailor. The shop was rebuilt in the 1950s on its former site, but further back from the original building line to give a wider pavement. By then it had been taken over by Matthes.

King Street, looking north, *c.* 1947. The buildings to the left have all been demolished and replaced by modern council flats.

No. 51 King Street, 1944. This building was the Labour Club. Note the door on the right, leading to the cellar, which was used as an air-raid shelter.

Regent Street, looking east, late 1870s. The post office sign can be seen next to the private house on the left. The house was taken up later by the post office in 1913 to enlarge its premises. The elegant costumes of the day can clearly be seen on the right. Great Yarmouth once boasted a unique system of narrow alleys, known by its inhabitants as rows. At least 156 of these rows ran east to west and for any large vehicle wishing to transverse the town in the same direction, routes were somewhat limited. The two main exceptions were Fullers Hill at the north end of the town, and Friars Lane at the southern end. The Broad and Market Rows could be used to provide limited access. Posts were erected in the Market Row in 1784 to prevent this. A new more central route was needed. Regent Street was opened to the public on 29 September 1813. Regent Street soon became an important thoroughfare giving an ideal route from the Quay to King Street and Market Place.

King Street, 1937. Charles Bosket's baker's shop is to the far left, with the west end of Row 86 between that and the impressive house with the bay and large tree in the garden. Dr Wyllys, a local doctor, lived at no. 25 for many years. The shop to the right, with the extended blind, was that of Richard Bratton, music seller. A few months after this photograph was taken, Dr Wyllys's house and the buildings to the right were demolished to build a new row of shops.

King Street, looking towards St George's Church, 1939. Note the car registration number, EX4501, and the fully loaded wheelbarrow. The earth piled up by the side of the church is from air-raid trench material.

SECTION TWO

PUBLIC HOUSES

The Railway Tavern, 33 North Quay, c. 1923. This public house stood on the north-west corner of the Conge. It was formerly the Dolphin, then later the Railway Terminus. In a directory for 1905 it is listed as 'the North Quay Distillery', with yet another change of sign by the 1920s to the Railway Tavern. This is typical of the kaleidoscopic change of names necessary to keep pace with topical trends and events. Note the landlord's name above the doorway, William Holland.

The Bull Hotel, on the corner of Market Place and Market Gates, 1864. The hotel closed in 1911, and the premises were sold to Arthur Hollis, who traded there for many years. The building was finally demolished in the early 1970s and a modern shop was built on the site.

Market Tavern, Market Place, *c.* 1870. This was formerly called the Jolly Butchers, then the Fish Stall and by 1863 the Market Tavern. The sign was changed back to the Fish Stall (House) in the 1890s. It closed in 1971 and a year later was demolished to make way for the Market Gates development.

The Distillery, 40 Market Place, *c.* 1922. John Rich reigned as landlord from around 1908 until the early 1930s. The building was rebuilt in 1831, when it was the Elephant and Castle. Row 58 is to the left.

The Red House, 1960s. The Distillery's sign was by 1934 changed to the Market Distillery. Local people had a nickname for the pub, 'The Red House'. In the late 1950s the name 'Red House' began to appear in directories. At a later date Palmer's took over the old pub and ran a gift shop, before it was finally demolished to make way for Downsway supermarket (see vol. 1, p. 32).

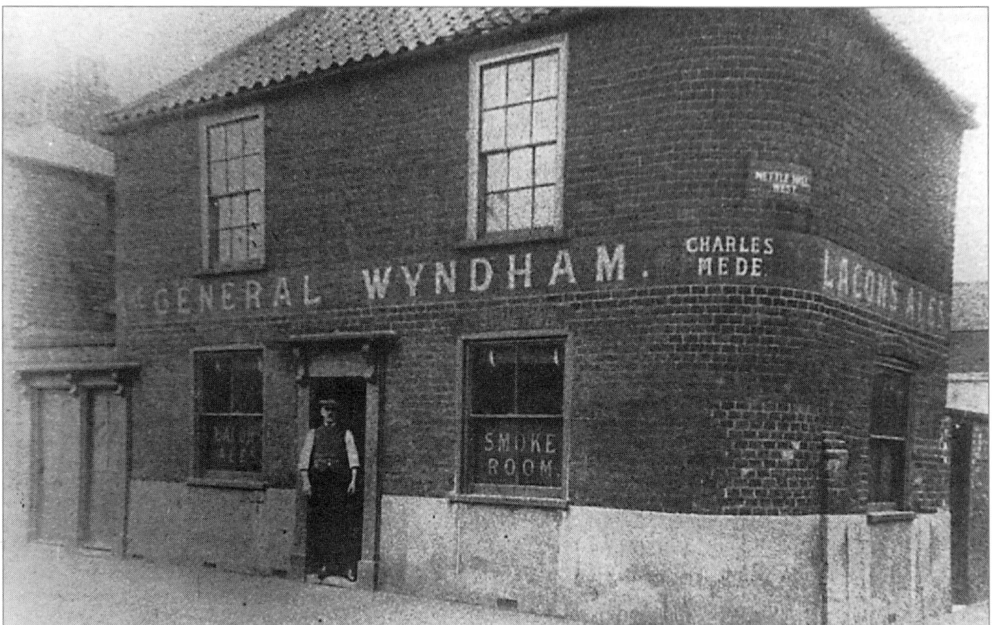

General Wyndham, Nettle Hill West, *c.* 1922. This building still stands today and is now in use as a private house. The old doorway, in which the landlord Mr Mede is seen standing, has been bricked up. The scar of the door can be picked out in the cement rendering.

Market Gates House, 5 Market Gates, *c.* 1923. In line with this old house, many of these small pubs closed in the early 1930s. A small car park covers the site today. The shop to the far left, then the Co-op Bakers, is today a fish shop.

The Enterprise, 30 Howard Street South, 1920s. Row 80 is just in view to the right.

Rodney Tavern, 13 Rodney Road, 1922. Today this is a private house. The arched windows can still be seen, but the doorway, once proclaiming 'George Osborne', the landlord, has long since disappeared.

Nursery Tavern, 101 Northgate Street. Between the upper second and third windows is a date stone: 'J. Yaxley, Nursery Place, 1872'. A directory for 1874 gives John Yaxley as a fish merchant and horse dealer. The Nursery Tavern is also noted, the landlord being James Hunt at the time. Market Gardens occupied the site in the 1850s. The building is still in use as Weldon's greengrocer's shop.

Queen Victoria, 156 Northgate Street, 1923. The landlady's name is above the door: Mrs Maud Artis. By the 1930s the premises had become a shop. Today it trades as Paul's butcher's shop. The old pub front can still be picked out among the brickwork.

St John's Head, North Quay. The teak front of Victorian design and the cement rendering have been removed to disclose much of the original and interesting brickwork. When the property was acquired by Lacon's in 1787 the rateable value was just £6.

Camperdown Tavern, 78 Nelson Road Central, *c.* 1922. This building is still in use today as a private house. The large doors, behind the lady to the right, have been bricked up and a modern doorway and window added. However, the old pub front has survived and can easily be picked out.

The Rifle Volunteer public house, 12 Dene Side, *c.* 1923. The landlord's name, Walter Bugg, is clearly visible on the sign. The building still stands today, although no longer a pub, but a private residence.

Suspension Bridge Tavern, Bridge Road, 1922. This old Lacon's pub has been modernized over the years, but has kept its traditional appearance and charm.

The Eastern Star, on the corner of Middle Market Road and Union Road, mid-1920s. The landlord, Arthur Hallums, is in the doorway.

Prince Of Wales Tavern, 114 Nelson Road Central, 1923. In the 1960s the premises were taken over by Boardley and Roberts, electrical wholesale dealers. In more recent years it traded as a carpet shop. Sadly, today, this once proud public house stands empty, its fate unknown.

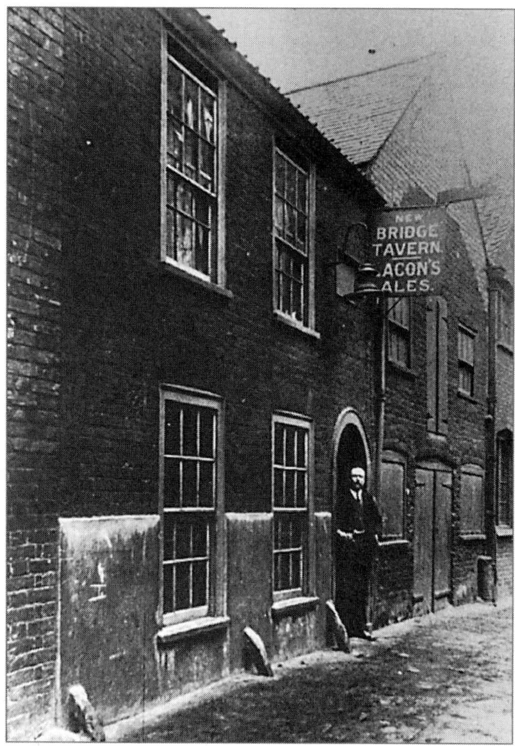

New Bridge Tavern, Steam Mill Road, 1920s. The buildings to the right still exist today. The public house is long gone and the site is now a car sales yard.

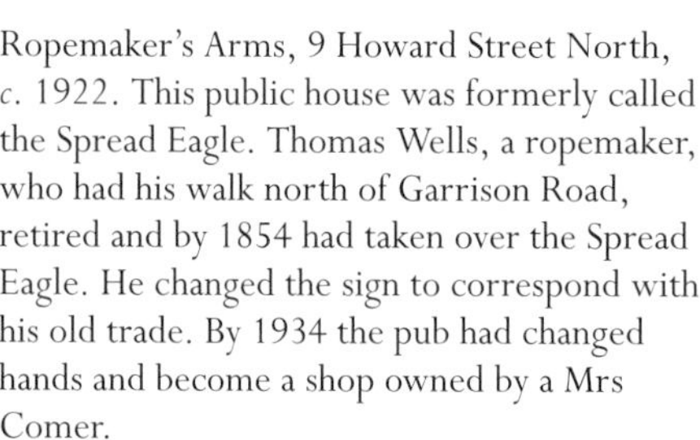

Ropemaker's Arms, 9 Howard Street North, *c.* 1922. This public house was formerly called the Spread Eagle. Thomas Wells, a ropemaker, who had his walk north of Garrison Road, retired and by 1854 had taken over the Spread Eagle. He changed the sign to correspond with his old trade. By 1934 the pub had changed hands and become a shop owned by a Mrs Comer.

The George and Dragon, 12 Church Plain, 1923. The landlord, David Hollis, is standing in the doorway. Just to the right is the butcher's shop of Mr Boothby. Row 12 is to the left of the pub.

Blackfriars Tavern, 94 Blackfriars Road, *c.* 1922. The boxed out wooden front has been bricked up, but little else has changed over the years. A drainpipe to the side of the building is marked with the date 1898.

Tanners' Arms, 5 Union Road, 1922. Note the poster advertising the Central Cinema (see vol. 1, p. 34) behind the landlord, Mr Brooks.

The Belvidere, 29 Kitchener Road, 1922. The landlord of 1869 was Thomas Clements. Kitchener Road was then known as Cemetery Road. In the mid-1960s the old pub was converted into flats, but the outline of the original building can still easily be seen.

Section Three

Shopfronts

Mr Robert Parker's bread shop, 47 Blackfriars Road (37 Tower Road), 1890s. The baker's barrow is parked in Abyssinia Road. Note the price of bread in the window – 2d a loaf. Sadly the number of these old corner shops has dwindled over the years. Nowadays, larders and fridges are usually well stocked, most items having been purchased at supermarkets.

Palmer Bros', Market Place. The decorative display is part of the celebrations for Queen Victoria's Diamond Jubilee in 1897.

David McCowan's tailor's shop, 37 Regent Street, *c.* 1903. Today, Loveland's estate agents offers its services from these premises.

Thomas Warren Estate Agency, 38 Regent Street, *c.* 1896. This single-storey building still survives today and houses Smith's cleaners. To the right, just in view, is no. 37, James Ellis, again a tailor's.

Howlett Smith's, jeweller and watchmaker, 28 Regent Street, 1909. This photograph was taken just after the owner had moved from the Broad Row. To the right is J. Girling, coal merchants, and on the other side of the shop, just in view, at no. 29 is the sign for another coal merchants, Bessery and Palmer. Note the large lamps outside the shop windows.

Alfred Moss's shops, 33–35 St Peter's Road, *c.* 1905. No. 33 traded as a restaurant on the ground floor, with dining rooms above. Note the waiter looking out of the window. Next, at no. 34, was the floral, fruit and vegetable section. The fish and poultry department followed on at no. 35 with supper rooms above.

Pagano's, confectioner, 68 Blackfriars Road. Sadly, in recent years this sweet shop finally closed its doors to those children who spent their occasional coppers on aniseed balls, liquorice ladders, dolly mixtures, gobstoppers and such like. Mr Pagano is on the far right in his white coat.

Robert Eastoe's shop, 133 Mill Road, Cobholm. The premises are decorated for the coronation of George VI in 1937. Queens Place is to the left.

Rogers' Criterion Hotel, Church Plain, *c.* 1892. Rogers proved popular with its 1*s* dinners, as advertised in the windows. By the turn of the century Bretts had taken over the premises (see vol. 1, p. 76).

Valentine Andrews, plumber and decorator, 11 Northgate Street. In prewar days these old craftsmen took great pride in their work and laboured very long hours.

Star Supply Stores, 111 King Street. It was from stores such as this that the weekly provisions were bought. The assistants would weigh and fold the blue bags of sugar. The amount of cheese requested was cut by a steel wire and again neatly wrapped. The bacon slicer had a big handle and a sound of its own as it cut the large joints of ham and meat, like those hanging outside this shop. The Maypole, Home and Colonial, and similar shops had a smell and atmosphere that could never be reproduced in the modern supermarket of today. Note the number of staff and, of course, the prices in the windows.

Robert Davis in the doorway of his shop, 59 King Street, early 1930s. In 1936 Mr Davis was listed as a furniture dealer, but noting his window and the signs above his shop he obviously sold everything from a violin to a bicycle. By 1938 David Richard had taken over the shop. Richard's still trades today and the shopfront has changed very little.

Jays Library, 142 King Street. The adverts for fireworks lead us to believe that this picture, and the one above, were taken in about November. Mrs Friend managed this business for quite some years. Note the fine sign advertising London coaches close to the young lady in the doorway.

Botwright's hairdressers, Theatre Plain, late 1960s. To the right is the Conservative Club. Just visible further along is the blind belonging to John Buckle's printers. In the early 1970s these buildings were all demolished to make way for the Market Gates development.

Arnold's furniture depository, Theatre Plain, 1920s. This is possibly a sale day as a large queue has formed, waiting for the doors to open. The door of the Blue Coat Bazaar is opposite on the left.

John Platten, fish merchant. Mr Platten traded from the corner of Market Gates and the Market Place in the 1920s. In more recent years the newsagent Strickland's occupied the premises, which were demolished in 1972 to make way for the Market Gates development.

Frank Base, pork butcher, 131 Mill Road, Cobholm, *c.* 1915. These were the days when pork sausages cost 8*d* a pound and beef 6*d*. Researchers beware: the numbering has changed on Mill Road.

The corner of Regent Road and King Street, just before the turn of the century. The shop with the clock in the background is situated in King Street. Mr Last's name is over the door, but by this time another jeweller, Lewis and Borne, had taken over. By 1904 Yarmouth's best known jewellers, Aldred's, had moved in. The premises were rebuilt when the Arcade was erected in 1924. Tom Greens was situated on the opposite corner. Locals always refer to this area as 'Tom Greens Corner'. At 14a King Street, next door, Mrs Miller, a photographer and fine art dealer, had her shop. By 1904 Alfred Yallop, a Gorleston photographer, had taken over this business. In more recent years Matthes the bakers had a shop on these premises.

Nos 18–20 Blackfriars Road, 1974. Shortis, seen to the left, sold car spares. The small cottage next door had a charm all of its own. The Rifle Volunteer public house called 'time gentlemen please' for the last time in August 1974. Soon after, these three buildings were demolished and sadly another part of the old town vanished.

No. 157 Nelson Road Central. This was William Chapman's fishmonger's shop. It still stands today as a solarium, called the Sun Shack but is now no. 153.

SECTION FOUR

QUAYS

South Quay looking south, 1870s. The front of the old Town Hall, which faced west, is in the foreground. This grand building was replaced by the present Town Hall in 1882. What an imposing sight the quay must have been. It was, in places, 100 yards wide, and for almost its entire length it was tree lined. Here fine vessels moored – not the ugly coasters and shipping of today, but fine four-masted barques and sailing ships of all descriptions. Movement and atmosphere were seen from the bridge to the south gate.

The Town Hall and Hall Quay, 1920s. Note the First World War tank (by the building on the left), which was presented to the town in 1919. It was placed on show outside the post office on Hall Quay. When the tank became rusty a citizen of the town offered to paint it, but in 1923 it was removed and probably went for scrap. Just in view to the left are the public lavatories. The old tram lines are also visible.

Hall Quay, 1917. This is not the tank described above. In fact it was a tramcar, which was disguised as a tank as part of the war effort to sell War Savings Certificates. Note both the Buck Inn and the Barge Tavern in the background.

The Town Hall, 1887. In 1886 the new Town Hall started to sink at the west end (see vol. 1, p. 39). The solution was found by an engineer, Mr Duckham, with the use of screw piles. The large girders shown here were placed under the tower, which weighed 700 tons.

The Assembly Rooms, 1887. The scaffolding was used at the Assembly Rooms to shore up and cradle the walls while the building was being raised.

Hall Quay, *c.* 1965. Note the 'For Sale' sign on the Central Library, which by this time had moved into the new premises in Tolhouse Street. Today the building is occupied by Aldred's estate agents.

Mr Clowes' grocer's shop, Hall Quay, *c.* 1897. A grocery business on this site can be traced back to 1787, when William Morgan purchased the premises. John Clowes had taken over by 1845 and the firm traded on Hall Quay up until the Second World War.

The Yare public house, Hall Quay, mid-1970s. At this time the property was looking very sorry for itself. In 1978 it was purchased by the Midland Bank.

Statues outside unknown house on The Conge. These two figures later stood outside Steward and Patteson's, Brewery premises on North Quay. They were originally placed each side of the doorway, but as a result of vandalism in 1961 they were moved above the doorway. These statues, which have been called by some the 'gardener and his wife', vanished after the building was demolished in the early 1970s.

The opening of the temporary Haven Bridge, while the present bridge was being built, 1928. The mayor's car is about to be driven over the bridge by the mayor himself, accompanied by the town clerk and the commissioners' clerk. After their return over the old bridge, it was declared closed.

The White Swan public house, 32 South Quay, 1922. Row 118 is to the right of the inn. A sign above the row is advertising Sharman and Co., basket makers, which had its works in this row. The shop at no. 31, to the left, was Mr Seaman's hairdresser's shop.

Vauxhall Railway Bridge, North Quay, 18 May 1901. The children are awaiting the return of the volunteers from the Boer War.

The Bure Bridge, 1890s. This photograph was taken long before the peace and tranquillity of this area was ruined by the A47 (see vol. 1, p. 103).

The Bure Bridge, looking north-east, 1937. Note the Tolhouse on the east side, used at that time as a boot repair shop. The Malthouses, used by Lacons on Rampart Road, are in the background.

A temporary bridge erected in 1953. By 1933 the old suspension bridge was found to be inadequate for modern traffic. A weight restriction was enforced, sending even more traffic on to the nearby railway bridge. The correct name for a bridge of this type is a Callender Hamilton bridge. The approach road can still be seen today.

The Callender Hamilton bridge being demolished, early 1970s. The present bridge, a concrete structure, was opened in 1972.

South Quay, between Queen Street and Row 92, during the Second World War. Note the bomb damage to these buildings, which were once fine merchants' houses.

South Quay during the Second World War. The buildings pictured above are to the extreme left. Row 96 was situated to the left of the building with the pillars. Today, Yarmouth Way comes through to South Quay at this point. The building just to the left of Row 96 had to be demolished.

The picturesque South Quay, looking south, *c*. 1867. Note the three men standing with the young boy by the barrow in the foreground. The quayside looks very busy with all of the ships moored alongside.

South Quay, 1870s. Note the crane unloading at the quayside. Sadly the days of sails have gone, and beautiful South Quay is now choked with modern-day traffic.

The Upper Ferry Inn, 50 South Quay, showing bomb damage. To the left of the pub is Row 136, which had been closed at the west end. These buildings were demolished after the Second World War. Council flats now occupy the site.

The Upper Ferry in much happier days before the Second World War. The landlord, William Gedge, has an array of plants decorating the pub.

SECTION FIVE

MARKET PLACE

Market Place, late 1920s. Note the tram lines on the west side, which originally, when laid in 1902, were single track. In 1913 the line was converted into double track. Sadly, today almost all of the fine buildings seen on the east side have been demolished. Yarmouth Market in its heyday was a wonderful sight. It comprised six rows of stalls, displaying home-grown produce from farms, market gardens, flower growers, butchers and other produce from the country. Like all markets, Yarmouth also had its cheap jacks and china stalls. There was always a book stall, stocking stall, sweet stall, tea stalls and, of course, the famous Yarmouth chip stalls.

Palmer's store, 1891. Palmer's has had a store in the Market Place for well over 150 years (see vol. 1, p. 36). Garwood Palmer, the founder, was said to be handsome, persuasive, fond of a joke and smartly dressed. He was recognized as the typical gentleman draper. Since those early days the firm has seen steady expansion. This photograph was taken just before the purchase of no. 37. Row 54 is just in view to the right.

Palmer's store, 1892. By this time no. 37 had become part of the main store. The east end of Row 51½ is to the far right. Row 54 is situated beneath the word 'carpet' on the shop sign. To the left of the store is the end of Row 56.

Palmer's store, 1904. In December 1892 a fire destroyed most of the store. Nos 38 and 39 were rebuilt, but no. 37 escaped damage. This photograph shows the rebuilt part with no. 37 still standing proudly at the north end.

Palmer's store, 1902. The shop has been decorated for the coronation of King Edward VII. The tower waggon, to the right, is in use fixing the overhead wires for the new electric tram service, which opened the same year.

A busy scene outside Palmer's at the turn of the century. Note the lamps outside the windows. A covered arcade in Row 54 had been added, with windows on both sides.

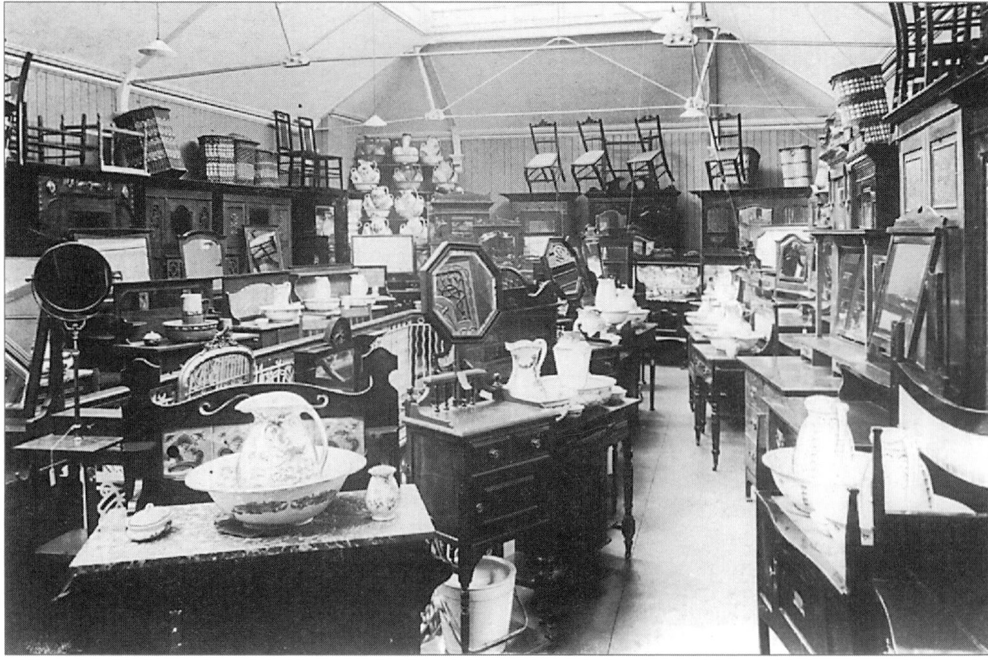

The interior of Palmer's, 1907. This photograph shows the furniture department.

Palmer's store, 1919. In 1910 no. 37 was demolished and a new bay and the tower were built. This is much as the store looks today. The decorations are for peace-day celebrations after the First World War.

Palmer's store, 1937. Note the shop's arcade-like windows. In this year the department store was 100 years old.

Palmer's store. A staff dinner at the Goode's Hotel, Marine Parade, 1937, held to celebrate 100 years of trading.

Palmer's office. This is where all of those small tube-like containers were sent, holding the purchase cash, via a network of pipes round the store. The young lady would then check the money and send the required change back.

Palmer's men's shop, 1950s. Row 60 is to the left of the shop, with Timothy White's hardware store on the other side of the row. Palmer's always had a good reputation for quality and service, and still trades along the same lines today. Girls were trained in all departments, and it was a recommendation to have worked there.

Market Place, looking north, early 1870s. Palmer's large windows are to the left. This photograph was taken before the purchase of no. 38. The sign of no. 34, Jolly and Harrison grocer's shop, is also visible.

Market Place, *c*. 1948. Purdy's was a well-known food and delicatessen shop, and it also had a fine restaurant. The shop was sold in 1972 for the sensational price of £207,000. Cooper's the ironmongers is next door but one, with the blinds out. This is followed by the International grocery stores on the corner of the Market Row. Purdy's is today the home of the Halifax Building Society and Cooper's Hughes TV.

Norman's 13/14 Market Place. Simon Norman opened his first shop in a row off Blind Howard Street in 1820. By 1859 he had moved to 14 Market Place, with a further purchase of no. 13 in 1904. The shopfront is pictured before alterations took place in the early 1960s. The family has been trading for well over 170 years, still supplying the town with fine furniture.

Nos 14–17 Market Place, July 1975. On the right is Norman's, with its modern shopfront. It is followed by three empty shops. No. 15b was Telefusion Ltd TV rentals. Next door is Express Cleaners. REC tile shop, with its sign, was on the corner of Row 29. The King's Head, now renamed the Market Tavern, is to the far left.

The Charity School, on the corner of the Market Place and Theatre Plain, 1880s. This school was founded in 1713, but the Market Place buildings date from 1724. In 1854 the school had 100 boys and 50 girls. The entrance to the school was in Theatre Plain. The figures of the boy and girl in the niches were given to the Towns Museum in 1892, but sadly they were destroyed when the Tolhouse was bombed in 1941. The school closed in 1891 and the children were transferred to the Hospital School. By 1896 it had become the Old Blue Coat Bazaar, and in more recent years it was Nichol's Restaurant. The building was finally demolished in the early 1970s to make way for the Market Gates development.

Procession for the coronation of King George V, 1911. Many tea parties were held in the Rows, and a huge bonfire was built on Gorleston Cliffs.

The procession above turning into Regent Street. Arnolds is to the left with Boning's large department store on the right.

Fair time in Yarmouth Market Place. Note the Two Necked Swan public house in the background.

Until recent years, The Mat was always a feature of Yarmouth's fair.

Steward and Son, chemist, 5 Market Place. The name Steward, as a chemist on this site, goes back to at least 1830 with a Charles Steward. The columns, which were once a feature of this shop, were fitted in the 1870s. Row 20 is to the left. The chemist's shop traded, using the same name, until the late 1980s. Today the premises are used as a restaurant.

The north end of the Market Place, 1870s. One of the market pumps is visible. This stood almost opposite the end of today's Conge.

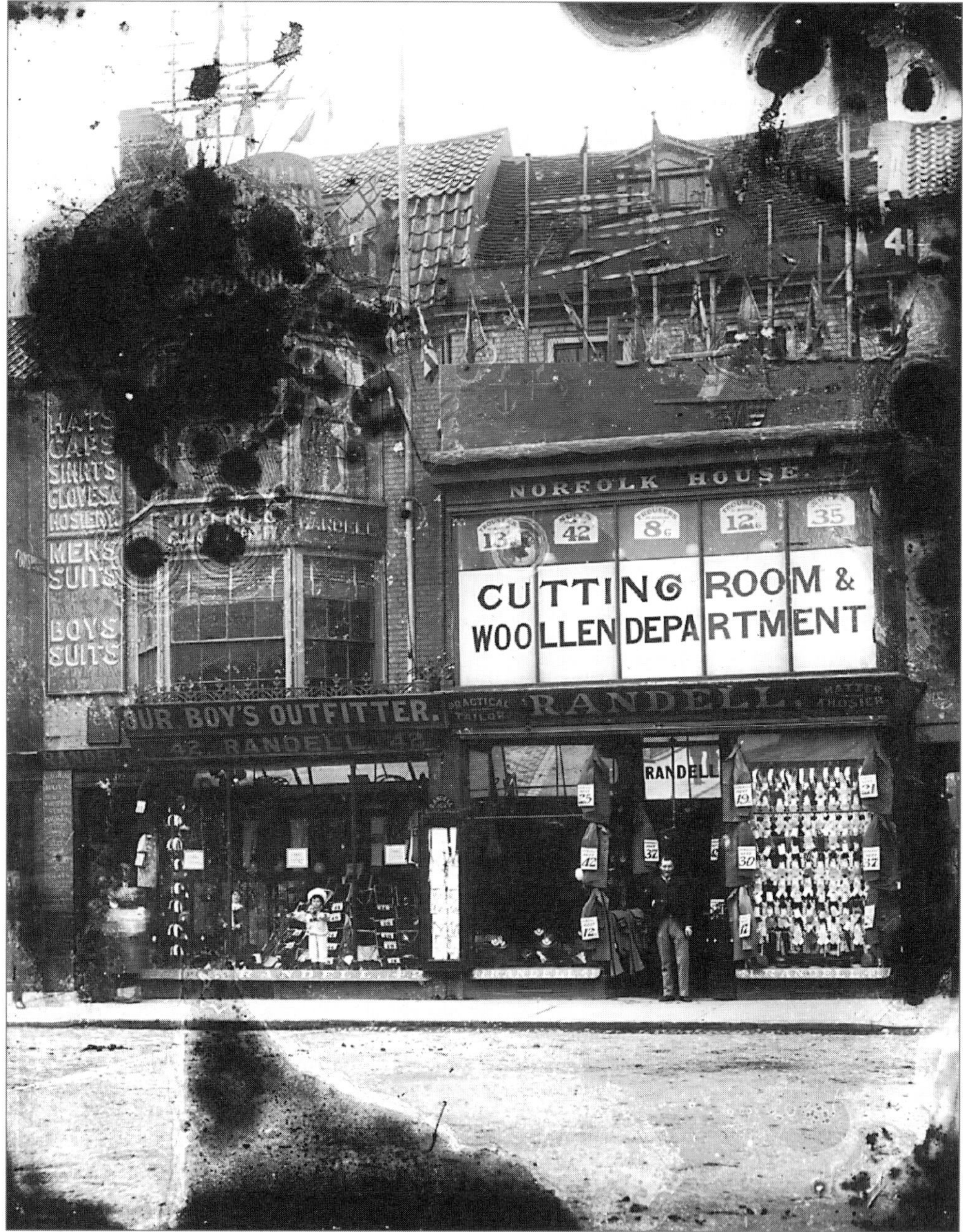

Mr Randall's shop, 41/42 Market Place, 1890s. This print was made directly from the old glass plate, which was rescued from the dustbin, along with many others, by Mr Barry Daniels. Although damaged, it is still a wonderful view of a Market Place shop. It might easily have been lost for ever (see vol. 1, p. 35).

Section Six

MISCELLANY

Fullers Hill, 1934. This was one of many street parties that were held to celebrate the Yarmouth carnival. Wheatley's shop and the Crystal pub are the only original buildings left today. For road-widening purposes the demolition of the houses commenced in around 1937. The remaining buildings followed in the early 1970s.

Market Row, looking west, 1922. Mr Bond's toy and fancy bazaar is to the left. The signs on the right advertised Hepworth's at no. 20, followed by William Reade's china shop next door.

Market Row, looking east, 1922. In the left foreground, Walter Carr's draper's shop window is crammed with clothes. In the 1930s the shop became Brant's, but in 1938 it was destroyed by fire. In September 1995 the rebuilt store, now Court's furniture shop, together with other premises, suffered the same fate.

Yarmouth Hospital, Dene Side, opened in 1839. This hospital was supported by voluntary contributions. A new hospital was opened by Sir James Paget on this site in 1888. With the opening of the Sir James Paget Hospital in Gorleston in 1982, the old site was finally sold.

Yarmouth Hospital, 1939. The sandbags in front of the building are to give it some protection from war damage (see vol. 1, p. 125).

Garage on the corner of Cobbs Place and Middlemarket Road, 1920s. The Co-operative Society shops, with their blinds out, are on the left. Note the petrol pump on the corner of the garage and the clock on the Co-op stores (see vol. 1, p. 82).

By the early 1930s the above garage had been demolished and replaced by the Co-op's new milk dairy. This was fitted out with the latest dairy equipment. The building had a frontage of some 44 feet long, impressively fitted out with four huge plate-glass windows.

The interior of the dairy showing the bottle washer. The public could view the whole process of cleaning to bottling the milk from the pavement outside. The building was lined throughout with white glazed bricks and tiles.

The dairy equipment had the capacity to deal with 400 gallons of milk per hour. My late father worked as a milkman from this dairy for many years and I have fond memories of the building.

Archway Cottages, Blackfriars Road, *c.* 1939. Sadly these buildings have all been demolished. Yarmouth's ancient town wall, standing to the rear of the buildings, has been revealed, and the area has been tidied up and is now grassed over. It now presents one of the most magnificent stretches of the wall.

When the buildings in Blackfriars Road were cleared in the early 1970s, the town wall was exposed.

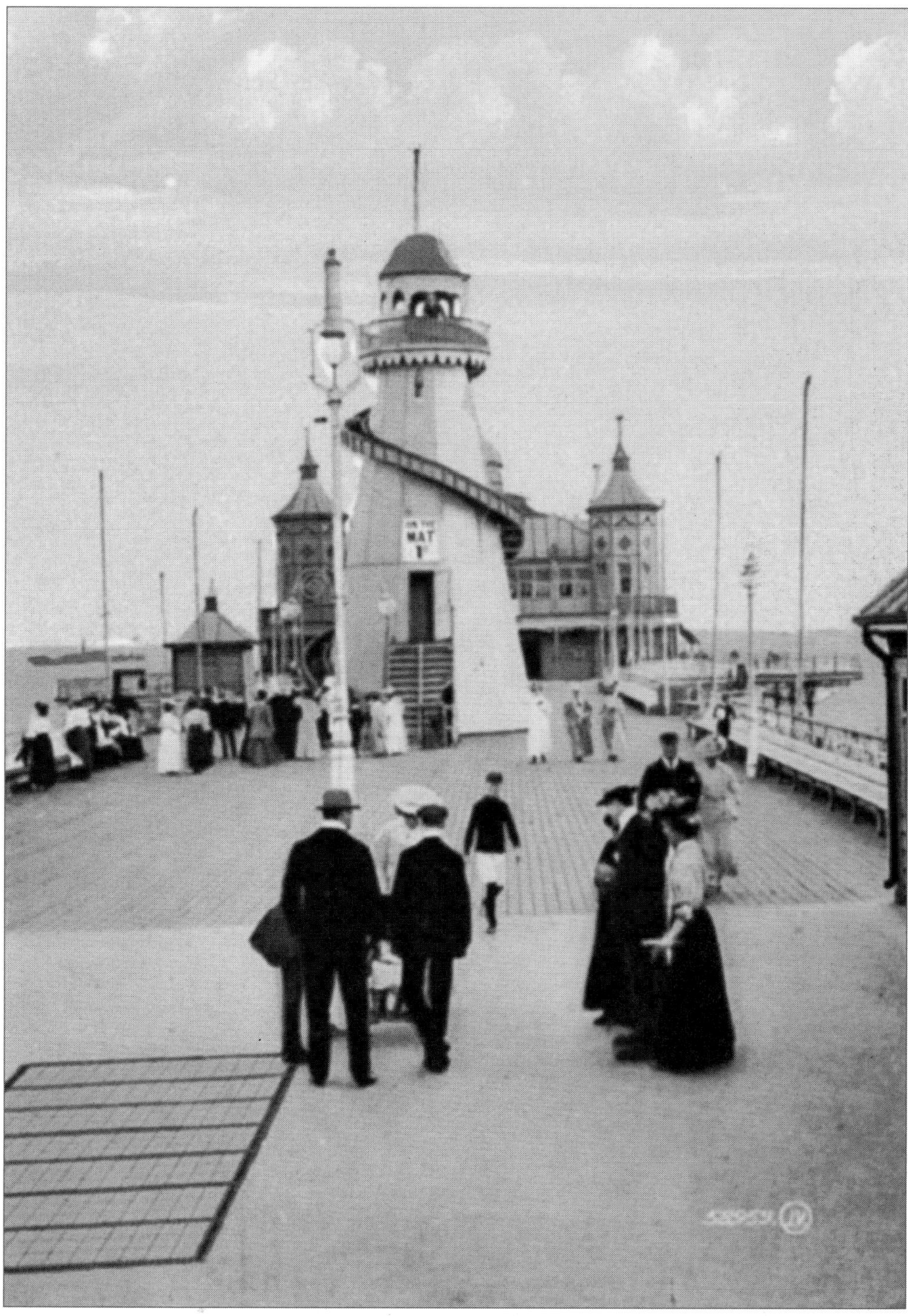

The Mat, Britannia Pier. The Mat first appeared here in about 1906. This postcard must date from before 1909 as we know that the Pavilion, to the rear, was destroyed by fire that year. After that date, no photograph has yet been found which includes The Mat; the top section of the helter-skelter survives today as a summer-house, standing by the river at Potter Heigham.

The Methodist Temple, Priory Plain. A date stone to the top of this Greek-style construction denotes 1875, the time of building. Unfortunately the building has been demolished and replaced by a roadway.

The Sunday School, which stood to the left of the temple, opened in 1855.

Jubilee Place, looking north. The plaque on the end house, no. 4, commemorated Queen Victoria's Golden Jubilee in 1887.

Jubilee Place, early 1970s. This photograph was taken just before its demolition to make way for the new Market Gates development.

Mr Munday on his milk round in Cobholm.

Platten's delivery van. Charlie Ebbage is to the left of the settee and the late Reg Emmerson is on the right.

The interior of a Maypole shop. A sign similar to the one at the rear, left corner – 'Maypole Dairy' – was found in the cellar of the Broad Row branch. Decorated for Christmas, this may in fact have been the Broad Row shop. The gentleman with the moustache has a likeness to the manager (standing in the doorway of the same shop, see vol. 1, p. 75).

Gorleston Garage in the 1920s, displaying a fine turn-out of early motor vehicles. A garage still trades on the site today.

Fullers Hill, 1955. The van is just about to pass Leonard Capon's general stores on the left, which is displaying the Walls sign above. The end of George Street can be seen on the same side, at the top of the hill.

SECTION SEVEN

GORLESTON

Royal Proclamation of Queen Elizabeth II, Gorleston High Street, Friday 8 February 1952. This photograph is part of a collection belonging to the late Frank Bell, who was an authority on Gorleston. I was privileged to have spent many an evening discussing with him his beloved Gorleston. I should like to dedicate this chapter to him as a small memorial.

Cliff Hill. Note the young boys standing outside no. 26, around the barrow which belonged to Bussey's grocers of Gorleston High Street.

Williams' the drapers on the corner of Bells Road and Upper Cliff Road, 1920s. A sign, reading 'Williams and Co Ltd', can still be seen in the doorway of the Lilac Box, a ladies' hairdressers, at 88 Upper Cliff Road, Gorleston.

German Zeppelin LZ127 off Gorleston, 1930s. This photograph, dated on the back 30 July 1931, was taken by Mrs Emms who lived at 3 Lowestoft Road. Looking down Sussex Road, the Zeppelin is seen going south providing a brilliant spectacle as she passes over. This airship was no stranger to the town. Her first appearance was in 1928, a month after she made her initial flight on 18 September 1928. A wonderful sight was afforded Gorleston people at about 9.10 in the evening, when the giant airship came along the coast from Lowestoft. The last recorded visit was in 1936 making, what at the time was said to be, a 'goodwill flight' over East Anglia. Was the real objective of the flight to observe British defences?

Parade of the local Gorleston 1914/18 war service volunteer reserves at the end of Church Road, near the White Horse public house.

Alfred Yallop, a photographer. His shop at 197/198 High Street, Gorleston, was on the corner of Priory Street. Moving from London, he started a business from these premises in the late 1880s. Photographers like Yallop and his son Sidney deserve our grateful thanks. The legacy left enables people like me to recall bygone days.

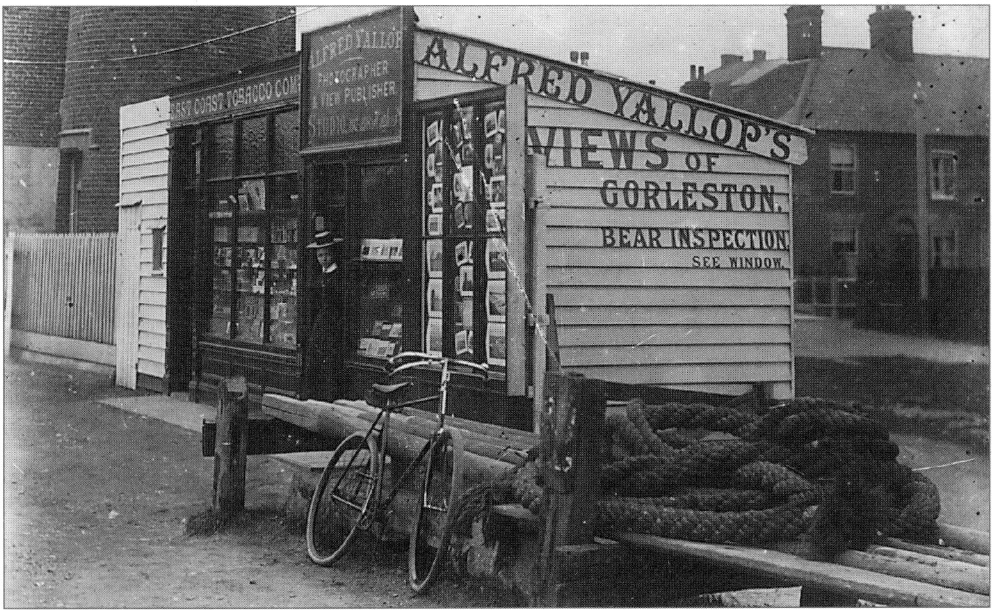

No. 17 Harbour Quay, Brush Wharf, 1905. By the turn of the century Alfred Yallop had opened this new branch. This was to cater for the holiday trade, which was at that time new to Gorleston. Harbour Terrace is in the background. The tobacconists shop of Joseph Liffen is to the left of Yallop's premises and is followed by the lighthouse.

Gorleston Beach, 1880s. The Cliff Hotel has not yet been built, which therefore dates this photograph to before 1898.

The Home Guard on Gorleston Beach, 1940.

Gorleston bandstand, *c.* 1923. This photograph evokes a very refined, lazy and peaceful Sunday afternoon. Sadly, it is a far cry from Gorleston Parade as it is today.

Beach and Gardens on a busy summer's day, late 1920s. Note the later built bandstand, which dates from 1924. A range of motor vehicles are parked with what appears to be hundreds of people out enjoying one of the hot summers we had in those days.

Gorleston Carnival, Quay Road, 4 July 1923. Carnivals years ago were something not to be missed and caused great excitement. Note the Bussey bicycle in the top picture.

The White Lion Inn on the corner of Cliff Hill and Upper Cliff Road. This photograph was taken prior to the rebuilding of this public house in 1897.

The Tramway Hotel, Lowestoft Road. This hotel took its name from the nearby terminus of the horse tram. It was built on the site of an earlier public house, the Horse and Groom. Work to build the hotel was started in 1875. It was originally to be called the Alexandra. The hotel was purchased by Lacon's in 1893. The tramway was destroyed by a direct hit during an air-raid in 1941, the occupants sadly being killed. The present-day tramway was built in 1956.

The buildings on the corner of Cross Road and High Street. This photograph was taken just before the demolition of these buildings to make way for the Palace Cinema, which was opened in 1939. Today it is used as a bingo hall.

Nos 139/140 High Street, just before the turn of the century. The sign over the gate, to the left, announces the residence of Dr Tipple. Barclays Bank occupies this site today. Next door at no. 140 was Gorleston post office. It moved to these premises in 1889. The two upper storeys were added in 1895.

Gorleston High Street, late 1960s. The Coliseum is to the left. Hammond's on the same side was soon to be taken over by Cooper's. Hollis's, one of the first self-service stores in Gorleston, is opposite.

The Electric Tramway, Gorleston station, opened in 1905, and the library, which opened in 1907. Both buildings were demolished to make way for the new library, which opened in 1974.

Cockrell's pork butcher's shop, 71 High Street, Gorleston, late 1920s. The window of this shop was always immaculate, as in this photograph.

Cockrell's other High Street shop, on the corner of Cross Road, 1930s. Frederick Cockrell died in 1936, when his son Bruce took over the business. Sadly, when Bruce died the butchery dynasty came to an end.

Bellamy's butcher's shop, Baker Street, Gorleston, *c.* 1907. Mr Bellamy is shown seated on his grand delivery cart, outside the premises. Note the then newly built Electric Tram station to the right of the shop.

The Co-operative shop on the corner of Beccles Road and Burgh Road, Gorleston, late 1960s. This photograph was taken just before the shop was demolished to make way for a large roundabout. The traffic lights also disappeared. Note the old police phone box on the corner of Burnt Lane.

Pier Plain, Gorleston, looking towards Baker Street, *c.* 1890. The building in the foreground to the right is the Ship public house, today known as Peggoty's. The next building, past the pair of bayfronted houses, has a datestone that reads, 'Goodwin Cottages 1882'. In the next row is another datestone, which reads 'Newman Cottages 1886'. The gable end of the house on the left still stands today, its window having been bricked up.

Bells Marsh Road, photographed during the floods of 1953. The night of 31 January 1953 saw the worst floods in living memory. Note the prefabs, which were built after the Second World War to rehouse people from war-torn Yarmouth.

Section Eight

Marine Parade

Marine Parade, Great Yarmouth, late 1870s. The Bath Hotel is on the left, followed by the two single-storey buildings, which were also part of the hotel. In 1903 these were demolished to enable the Circus to be seen from the parade. Note the tall beachman's lookout, which belonged to the Young and Diamond Company. Towering over the landscape, looking out to sea, this erection enabled an ever-watchful eye in the event of shipping in distress. Long ago this area was the domain of beachmen and fishermen. The present-day holiday industry was only founded in the mid-nineteenth century with the coming of the railways.

Marine Parade, mid-1870s. On the left, the building with the large door is a fish warehouse. Here they received the fish landed from the jetty and the beach. The fish were then packed and sent with all speed to the railways. This building still stands today, but is now hardly recognizable: it is an amusement arcade. Next door, on the corner of Lancaster Road, was the Telegraph Office. The Norfolk Hotel, formerly called The York, was opposite. The Young and Diamond lookout is in the background. The east end of York Road is followed by the sailors' home. The next five buildings had only recently been built.

Marine Parade, 1858. The Norfolk Hotel is to the left, near the lookout. The sailors' home is in the process of construction (note the pile of earth). The lifeboat station, next door, has only just been completed. The five buildings to the right of the sailors' home in the picture opposite are yet to be started. The second lookout to the right belongs to the Standard Company.

The sailors' home, early 1860s. Note the neat small walls around these buildings. The steps leading up to the lookout are clearly visible. These salvage companies were in existence long before the advent of the lifeboat. They used their yawls for rescuing shipwrecked sailors as well as for salvage.

The coastguard station, late 1860s. This was built in 1859 for the sum of £3,500. The building was demolished in 1964 to make way for the Tower Complex. To its left is the Royal Standard public house, with the lookout towering above. Just in view next door is Papworth's Windmill, which was demolished in 1881.

The Standard Company's lookout to the rear of the Royal Standard public house. The open doors of the lifeboat shed are to the left.

Small shop at the base of the Revolving Tower (see vol. 1, p. 73). Note the man to the left, with the words 'the Tower' on his cap. A sign pointing the way to the 'refreshment bar', shown below, is to the middle of the photograph.

The interior of the refreshment bar at the base of the tower. Note the prices on the menu board.

The Marine Arcade, 1920s. The twin turrets marking the entrances bear the dates 1902 and 1904 and are still visible today. More than thirty shops lined the glass-roofed arcade. Wixley the jewellers is to the far left, with Spall's fancy goods on the other side of the 1902 entrance. Palmer's had a branch to the left of the 1904 entrance, with the Arcade Restaurant on the opposite side. Sadly, today the arcade has been swallowed up by an amusement complex.

Marine Parade, looking north, July 1909. The 1904 arcade is seen to the left, but the Empire Cinema, which opened in 1911, has not yet been built.

Shoppers browsing in the Marine Arcade soon after it was built. Note the dolls in the window of the first shop on the left. Many well-known traders, sadly long gone, had small shops in this complex. Norton the tobacconists, Middleton's Bazaar, Keymer the fancy draper and even a palmist, Madame Sato, are just a few.

The pleasure beach, between 1925 and 1932. Among the stalls and rides, the Great Skidder sits in the foreground. The Ark in the background dates this photograph (see vol. 1, p. 72).

The miniature railway was once the favourite ride of every young budding engine driver.

Children enjoying a paddle in the warm seawater, just before the 1909 fire that resulted in the destruction of the pavilion on the Britannia Pier, which is visible here in the background.

Very early bathing machines on Yarmouth Beach. Victorian bathers were clothed in long 'reach me downs', extending from the neck to the ankle.

The bathing pool and jetty, 1930s (see vol. 1, p. 71).

Captured in this view of the Britannia Pier in the mid-1920s is, to the right, one of the three motor buses the corporation purchased second-hand from the London General Omnibus Company in 1925. It was the famous AEC B type. The other bus is a Guy BB type, purchased new to replace the Fishwharf Tram service and to commence one from Britannia Pier to Gorleston Beach.

Winton's Assembly Rooms, *c.* 1892. Most records indicate that this was formerly Berners House. In fact it was erected in the garden of that building. Berners House today is part of Barron's amusement arcade. The hotel was later taken over by John and William Goode, but in 1901 it was destroyed by fire (see vol. 1, p. 98).

The bar inside the Winton's Rooms.

Marine Parade, early 1870s. The Royal Hotel is in the middle with three bay windows. This photograph was taken before its rebuilding in the late 1870s. The single-storey building to the right was built by the Revd Charles Penrice and was named 'the Cabin'. It was demolished some years ago. The next building was erected in 1835 by William Bircham. Wellington Lodge stands on the corner of South Beach Place. The Royal Hotel stands today just as grand as it was when Dickens stayed there in 1848. The two large houses to the right also survive, with the ground floors turned into restaurants.

SECTION NINE

STIR THE MEMORY

This chapter consists of pictures to stir the memory. When and where were they taken? Are any of your family looking at us for recognition from this street party pictured above? It is possibly a coronation party in 1911.

A clearance area in the Rows, possibly off George Street.

A Yarmouth Row. The present generation is growing up surrounded by flats and wide streets. Once upon a time their fathers and grandfathers worked and lived in friendly rows such as this.

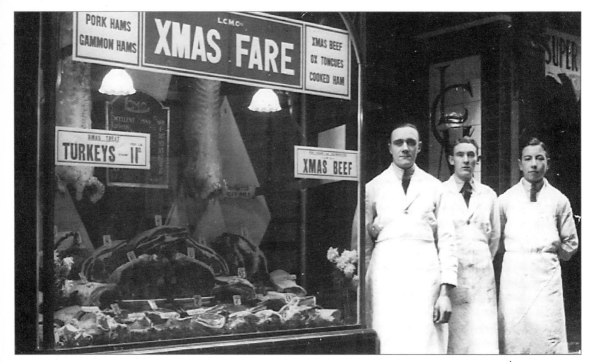

London Central Meat Co. Ltd. Was this the branch at 10 Market Row?

Mrs Watts and her son standing outside no. 14, Row 17 (18) in the early 1930s. The original Row 17 was demolished to make way for Lacon's Brewery extensions in 1895. The roadway, later no. 17, was wrongly numbered, this being the original Row 18, or Says Corner, South.

SECTION TEN

FIRES AND FLOODS

The Britannia Pier, 1932. The pier has suffered several fires and disasters since it was first built in 1858. At the time of this photograph the dance hall at the end of the pier was completely destroyed by fire. The pavilion in the background escaped damage. In one report a cigarette end was said to have caused the fire. The revolving tower is to the right.

The scene after the great fire at Arnold's department stores, looking east towards Boning's, 4 February 1919. Workmen are busy clearing the remaining walls, together with the stock which had been reduced to a heap of rubbish. The line of Row 66 can be seen to the right.

Arnold's store viewed from Regent Street after the fire.

Scenic railway fire, Sunday 6 April 1919. One would expect a construction of wood to blaze furiously, and this railway certainly did.

A Matthes' bread delivery van on fire on Gorleston Quayside.

The flooding of Hammond Road, August 1931.

Clarence Road, looking towards Blackfriars Road, 1953. At this time Yarmouth saw the worst floods in living memory. More than 3,500 houses were flooded by millions of gallons of seawater. By the time this photograph had been taken the water had started to recede. The Clarence Tavern is to the right, where two people are standing outside. Clarence Road was swept away in the redevelopment of the area in the 1970s.

ACKNOWLEDGEMENTS

Once again I am indebted to the many people who, over the years, have kindly loaned me their photographs, thus making this book a reality.

I must thank the staff of the Reference Library, Great Yarmouth, especially Michael Bean and Stella Cordingley, for their kind assistance; John Read and Peter Jones for their help and encouragement; Mr Sturrock of Palmer's for his help and allowing me to use their pictures; David Newman, Barry Daniels, John Read and Mr Watts for permission to reproduce their photographs; a special thanks to Mrs Hilary Freeman, daughter of the late Frank Bell (1914–95), local historian and authority on Gorleston – without his outstanding collection of photographs and notes, which I am proud now to have in my care, the chapter on Gorleston would never have materialized; to Mrs Joan Lobban I am indebted once again for, in difficult times, correcting my bad grammar. Finally, thanks go to my dear wife Susanne, not only for helping me to overcome a serious illness, but also for her great encouragement and wisdom. Without her this book would never have evolved.

BRITAIN IN OLD PHOTOGRAPHS

Aberystwyth & North Ceredigion
Around Abingdon
Acton
Alderney: A Second Selection
Along the Avon from Stratford to Tewkesbury
Altrincham
Amersham
Around Amesbury
Anglesey
Arnold & Bestwood
Arnold & Bestwood: A Second Selection
Arundel & the Arun Valley
Ashbourne
Around Ashby-de-la-Zouch
Avro Aircraft
Aylesbury
Balham & Tooting
Banburyshire
Barnes, Mortlake & Sheen
Barnsley
Bath
Beaconsfield
Bedford
Bedfordshire at Work
Bedworth
Beverley
Bexley
Bideford
Bilston
Birmingham Railways
Bishop's Stortford & Sawbridgeworth
Bishopstone & Seaford
Bishopstone & Seaford: A Second Selection
Black Country Aviation
Black Country Railways
Black Country Road Transport
Blackburn
Blackpool
Around Blandford Forum
letchley
olton
ournemouth
radford
aintree & Bocking at Work
recon
entwood
idgwater & the River Parrett
idlington
idport & the Bride Valley
ierley Hill
ighton & Hove
ighton & Hove: A Second Selection
stol
ound Bristol
xton & Norwood
ly Broadstairs & St Peters
mley, Keston & Hayes

Buckingham & District
Burford
Bury
Bushbury
Camberwell
Cambridge
Cannock Yesterday & Today
Canterbury: A Second Selection
Castle Combe to Malmesbury
Chadwell Heath
Chard & Ilminster
Chatham Dockyard
Chatham & Gillingham
Cheadle
Cheam & Belmont
Chelmsford
Cheltenham: A Second Selection
Cheltenham at War
Cheltenham in the 1950s
Chepstow & the River Wye
Chesham Yesterday & Today
Cheshire Railways
Chester
Chippenham & Lacock
Chiswick
Chorley & District
Cirencester
Around Cirencester
Clacton-on-Sea
Around Clitheroe
Clwyd Railways
Clydesdale
Colchester
Colchester 1940–70
Colyton & Seaton
The Cornish Coast
Corsham & Box
The North Cotswolds
Coventry: A Second Selection
Around Coventry
Cowes & East Cowes
Crawley New Town
Around Crawley
Crewkerne & the Ham Stone Villages
Cromer
Croydon
Crystal Palace, Penge & Anerley
Darlington
Darlington: A Second Selection
Dawlish & Teignmouth
Deal
Derby
Around Devizes
Devon Aerodromes
East Devon at War
Around Didcot & the Hagbournes
Dorchester
Douglas
Dumfries
Dundee at Work
Durham People

Durham at Work
Ealing & Northfields
East Grinstead
East Ham
Eastbourne
Elgin
Eltham
Ely
Enfield
Around Epsom
Esher
Evesham to Bredon
Exeter
Exmouth & Budleigh Salterton
Fairey Aircraft
Falmouth
Farnborough
Farnham: A Second Selection
Fleetwood
Folkestone: A Second Selection
Folkestone: A Third Selection
The Forest of Dean
Frome
Fulham
Galashiels
Garsington
Around Garstang
Around Gillingham
Gloucester
Gloucester: from the Walwin Collection
North Gloucestershire at War
South Gloucestershire at War
Gosport
Goudhurst to Tenterden
Grantham
Gravesend
Around Gravesham
Around Grays
Great Yarmouth
Great Yarmouth Revisited
Greenwich & Woolwich
Grimsby
Around Grimsby
Grimsby Docks
Gwynedd Railways
Hackney: A Second Selection
Hackney: A Third Selection
From Haldon to Mid-Dartmoor
Hammersmith & Shepherds Bush
Hampstead to Primrose Hill
Harrow & Pinner
Hastings
Hastings: A Second Selection
Haverfordwest
Hayes & West Drayton
Around Haywards Heath
Around Heathfield
Around Heathfield: A Second Selection
Around Helston
Around Henley-on-Thames

Herefordshire
Herne Bay
Heywood
The High Weald
The High Weald: A Second Selection
Around Highworth
Around Highworth & Faringdon
Hitchin
Holderness
Honiton & the Otter Valley
Horsham & District
Houghton-le-Spring & Hetton-le-Hole
Houghton-le-Spring & Hetton-le-Hole: A Second Selection
Huddersfield: A Second Selection
Huddersfield: A Third Selection
Ilford
Ilfracombe
Ipswich: A Second Selection
Islington
Jersey: A Third Selection
Kendal
Kensington & Chelsea
East Kent at War
Keswick & the Central Lakes
Around Keynsham & Saltford
The Changing Face of Keynsham
Kingsbridge
Kingston
Kinver
Kirkby & District
Kirkby Lonsdale
Around Kirkham
Knowle & Dorridge
The Lake Counties at Work
Lancashire
The Lancashire Coast
Lancashire North of the Sands
Lancashire Railways
East Lancashire at War
Around Lancaster
Lancing & Sompting
Around Leamington Spa
Around Leamington Spa: A Second Selection
Leeds in the News
Leeds Road & Rail
Around Leek
Leicester
The Changing Face of Leicester
Leicester at Work
Leicestershire People
Around Leighton Buzzard & Linslade
Letchworth
Lewes
Lewisham & Deptford: A Second Selection
Lichfield

Lincoln
Lincoln Cathedral
The Lincolnshire Coast
Liverpool
Around Llandudno
Around Lochaber
Theatrical London
Around Louth
The Lower Fal Estuary
Lowestoft
Luton
Lympne Airfield
Lytham St Annes
Maidenhead
Around Maidenhead
Around Malvern
Manchester
Manchester Road & Rail
Mansfield
Marlborough: A Second Selection
Marylebone & Paddington
Around Matlock
Melton Mowbray
Around Melksham
The Mendips
Merton & Morden
Middlesbrough
Midsomer Norton & Radstock
Around Mildenhall
Milton Keynes
Minehead
Monmouth & the River Wye
The Nadder Valley
Newark
Around Newark
Newbury
Newport, Isle of Wight
The Norfolk Broads
Norfolk at War
North Fylde
North Lambeth
North Walsham & District
Northallerton
Northampton
Around Norwich
Nottingham 1944–74
The Changing Face of Nottingham
Victorian Nottingham
Nottingham Yesterday & Today
Nuneaton
Around Oakham
Ormskirk & District
Otley & District
Oxford: The University
Oxford Yesterday & Today
Oxfordshire Railways: A Second Selection
Oxfordshire at School
Around Padstow
Pattingham & Wombourne

Penwith
Penzance & Newlyn
Around Pershore
Around Plymouth
Poole
Portsmouth
Poulton-le-Fylde
Preston
Prestwich
Pudsey
Radcliffe
RAF Chivenor
RAF Cosford
RAF Hawkinge
RAF Manston
RAF Manston: A Second Selection
RAF St Mawgan
RAF Tangmere
Ramsgate & Thanet Life
Reading
Reading: A Second Selection
Redditch & the Needle District
Redditch: A Second Selection
Richmond, Surrey
Rickmansworth
Around Ripley
The River Soar
Romney Marsh
Romney Marsh: A Second Selection
Rossendale
Around Rotherham
Rugby
Around Rugeley
Ruislip
Around Ryde
St Albans
St Andrews
Salford
Salisbury
Salisbury: A Second Selection
Salisbury: A Third Selection
Around Salisbury
Sandhurst & Crowthorne
Sandown & Shanklin
Sandwich
Scarborough
Scunthorpe
Seaton, Lyme Regis & Axminster
Around Seaton & Sidmouth
Sedgley & District
The Severn Vale
Sherwood Forest
Shrewsbury
Shrewsbury: A Second Selection
Shropshire Railways
Skegness
Around Skegness
Skipton & the Dales
Around Slough

Smethwick
Somerton & Langport
Southampton
Southend-on-Sea
Southport
Southwark
Southwell
Southwold to Aldeburgh
Stafford
Around Stafford
Staffordshire Railways
Around Staveley
Stepney
Stevenage
The History of Stilton Cheese
Stoke-on-Trent
Stoke Newington
Stonehouse to Painswick
Around Stony Stratford
Around Stony Stratford: A Second Selection
Stowmarket
Streatham
Stroud & the Five Valleys
Stroud & the Five Valleys: A Second Selection
Stroud's Golden Valley
The Stroudwater and Thames & Severn Canals
The Stroudwater and Thames & Severn Canals: A Second Selection
Suffolk at Work
Suffolk at Work: A Second Selection
The Heart of Suffolk
Sunderland
Sutton
Swansea
Swindon: A Third Selection
Swindon: A Fifth Selection
Around Tamworth
Taunton
Around Taunton
Teesdale
Teesdale: A Second Selection
Tenbury Wells
Around Tettenhall & Codshall
Tewkesbury & the Vale of Gloucester
Thame to Watlington
Around Thatcham
Around Thirsk
Thornbury to Berkeley
Tipton
Around Tonbridge
Trowbridge
Around Truro
TT Races
Tunbridge Wells

Tunbridge Wells: A Second Selection
Twickenham
Uley, Dursley & Cam
The Upper Fal
The Upper Tywi Valley
Uxbridge, Hillingdon & Cowley
The Vale of Belvoir
The Vale of Conway
Ventnor
Wakefield
Wallingford
Walsall
Waltham Abbey
Wandsworth at War
Wantage, Faringdon & the Vale Villages
Around Warwick
Weardale
Weardale: A Second Selection
Wednesbury
Wells
Welshpool
West Bromwich
West Wight
Weston-super-Mare
Around Weston-super-Mare
Weymouth & Portland
Around Wheatley
Around Whetstone
Whitchurch to Market Drayton
Around Whitstable
Wigton & the Solway Plain
Willesden
Around Wilton
Wimbledon
Around Windsor
Wingham, Addisham & Littlebourne
Wisbech
Witham & District
Witney
Around Witney
The Witney District
Wokingham
Around Woodbridge
Around Woodstock
Woolwich
Woolwich Royal Arsenal
Around Wootton Bassett, Cricklade & Purton
Worcester
Worcester in a Day
Around Worcester
Worcestershire at Work
Around Worthing
Wotton-under-Edge to Chipping Sodbury
Wymondham & Attleborough
The Yorkshire Wolds